Intimate Journals — Charles Baudelaire

Tu, la poudre est meilleure..
L'ailleurs, mêmes observations

Charles Baudelaire

INTIMATE
JOURNALS

Translated by

Christopher Isherwood

CITY LIGHTS BOOKS
San Francisco

First City Lights edition: March 1983

This translation was originally published in a limited edition by the Blackamore Press in 1930. Other editions have been published by Marcel Rodd, Inc. (1947), Methuen & Co., Ltd. (1949), and Beacon Press (1957).
Designed by Nancy J. Peters.

ISBN: 0-87286-147-3
ISBN: 0-87286-146-5 (pb)

Library of Congress Cataloging in Publication Data

Baudelaire, Charles, 1821-1867.
    Intimate journals.

    Translation of: Journaux intimes.
    Reprint. Originally published: Hollywood: M. Rodd, 1947.
    1. Baudelaire, Charles, 1821-1867—Biography.
2. Poets, French—19th century—Biography.
I. Title.
PQ2191.Z5A3413   1893   841'.8 (b)   83-5301
ISBN o-87286-146-5 (pbk.)

CITY LIGHTS BOOKS are edited by Lawrence Ferlinghetti & Nancy J. Peters and published at the City Lights Bookstore, 261 Columbus Avenue, San Francisco, California 94133.

TABLE OF CONTENTS

CONTENTS

ILLUSTRATIONS

What kind of a man wrote this book?

A deeply religious man, whose blasphemies horrified the orthodox. An ex-dandy, who dressed like a condemned convict. A philosopher of love, who was ill at ease with women. A revolutionary, who despised the masses. An aristocrat, who loathed the ruling class. A minority of one. A great lyric poet.

By nature, Baudelaire was a city-dweller. He was born (1821) and died (1867) in Paris. He loved luxury and fashionable splendor, the endless cavalcade of the boulevards, the midnight brilliance of talk in the artists' cafés. Paris taught him his vices, absinthe and opium, and the extravagant dandyism of his early manhood which involved him in debt for the rest of his life. Even in extreme poverty, he preferred the bohemian freedom of the Latin Quarter to the sheltered respectability of his family home. The atmosphere of Paris was the native element of his inspiration. He speaks of the 'religious intoxication of the great cities.' 'The pleasure of being in crowds is a mysterious expression of sensual joy in the multiplication of Number.'

Brussels, in the eighteen-sixties, was not a great city. It was a provincial town. Baudelaire hated it. Expressing his contempt for a man, he calls him 'a Belgian spirit.' But no doubt this attitude was also due to the state of his affairs and his health. Baudelaire did not come to Brussels until 1864, when he was already ruined, financially and physically. He was miserably poor. His work had failed to obtain proper recognition. Six of the poems in *Les Fleurs du Mal* had been judged obscene and suppressed by court order. His publisher had gone bankrupt. He was slowly dying of syphilis. Violent nervous crises made him dread insanity. 'Now I suffer continually from vertigo, and today, 23rd of January, 1862, I have received a singular warning. I have felt the wind of the wing of madness pass over me.'

Baudelaire was one of the first writers of 'the poetry of departure.' His longing for escape—from the Nineteenth Century and himself—fastened nostalgically upon ships. 'When,' he imagines them asking, 'shall we set sail for happiness?'

When Baudelaire was a boy of twenty, his parents became alarmed by the wildness of the life he was leading. They persuaded him to take a long ocean voyage, hoping that it would change his tastes and ideas. The ship was bound for Calcutta. Baudelaire insisted on leaving it at the island of Réunion and being sent back to France. He detested the sea and his fellow-passengers, but he never forgot this glimpse of the tropics. It is characteristic of him, and of the romantic attitude in general, that he later pretended to have been in India, told fantastic lies about his adventures, and always regretted the opportunity he had missed.

Shy men of extreme sensibility are the born victims of the prostitute. Baudelaire's mulatto mistress, Jeanne Duval, was a beautiful, indolent animal. She squandered his money and slept with his friends. The biographers usually condemn her; most unjustly. Few of us would really enjoy a love-affair with a genius. Jeanne had to endure Baudelaire's moods and listen to his poems; she understood neither. But, in some mysterious manner, these two human beings needed each other. They stayed together, on and off, for twenty years. Baudelaire always loved and pitied her, and tried to help her. Hideous and diseased, she limps out of his history on crutches and disappears.

Like many lesser writers before and after him, Baudelaire suffered constantly from Acedia, 'the malady of monks,' that deadly weakness of the will which is the root of all evil. He fought against it with fury and horror. 'If, when a man has fallen into habits of idleness, of day-dreaming and of sloth, putting off his most important duties continually till the morrow, another man were to wake him up one morning with heavy blows of a whip and were to whip him unmercifully, until he who was unable to work for pleasure worked now for fear—would not that man, the chastiser, be his benefactor and truest friend?' The *Intimate Journals* are full of such exclamations, coupled with resolves to work—'to work from six o'clock in the morning, fasting at midday. To work blindly, without aim, like a madman. . . . I believe that I stake my destiny upon hours of uninterrupted work.' It is terribly moving to read these passages, knowing that the time is close at hand when Baudelaire will be lying dazed and half-paralyzed; when he will no longer be able to remember his name and have to copy it, with tedious care, from the cover of one of his books; when he will not recognize his own face in the mirror, and will bow to it gravely, as if to a stranger.

In his lifetime, Baudelaire witnessed the dawn of the Steam Age—a false, gaslit dawn, loud with engines and advertisement, faithless, superstitious and blandly corrupt. Baudelaire foresees the future with dismay and denounces it in the magnificent outburst which opens with the words: 'The world is about to end. . . .' Elsewhere he writes: 'Theory of the true civilisation. It is not to be found in gas, or steam, or table-turning. It consists in the diminution of the traces of original sin.' After two world-wars and the atomic bomb, we of today should understand him better than his contemporaries.

Baudelaire's nervous, unstable temperament, his contempt for bourgeois ethics and his impatience of mediocrity led him into a series of quarrels—with his family, his friends and his business associates. For his mother—the only important woman in his life except Jeanne Duval—he experienced mingled feelings of love, exasperation, pity, rebellion and hatred. He sincerely admired his distinguished stepfather, General Aupick; but the two men were worlds apart, they spoke different languages and could never understand each other. He could appreciate the honesty and good-faith of Ancelle, his legal guardian; but the elderly lawyer's primness and caution drove him frantic. Even in middle age, Baudelaire often seems touchingly immature, like a defiant schoolboy surrounded by disapproving grown-ups.

His passionate outbursts and bitter words hurt nobody so much as himself. His rage was immediately followed by remorse. His last years were darkened with regrets—regrets for deeds done and undone, for health and vigor lost, for time irretrievably wasted. Yet Baudelaire never gave way finally to despair. He struggled with himself to the very end, striving and praying to do better. His life is not the dreary tale of a talented weakling, it is the heroic tragedy of a strong man beset by great failings. Even its horrible closing scenes should not disgust or depress us. They represent a kind of victory. Baudelaire died undefeated—a warning and an inspiration to us all.

The *Intimate Journals* consist of papers which were not collected and published until after Baudelaire's death. The section called *Squibs* was probably written before 1857; *My Heart Laid Bare* belongs, more or less, to the Brussels period. This latter title is taken from the writings of Edgar Allan Poe, who says that if any man dared to write such a book, with complete frankness, it would necessarily be a masterpiece. Baudelaire certainly dared, but he did not live to carry out his project. What we have here is an assortment of wonderful fragments, cryptic memoranda, literary notes, quotations, rough drafts of prose poems, explosions of political anger and personal spleen.

After some thought, I have decided not to attempt annotation. I have neither the time nor the scholarship for such a task—and, anyway, what does it matter to the average reader who Moun was, or Castagnary, or Rabbe? Read this book as you might read an old diary found in the drawer of a desk in a deserted house. Substitute—if you like—names from your own life and world, names of friends and enemies, of band-wagon journalists and phony politicians. Much of the obscurity is unimportant or on the surface. The more you study these *Intimate Journals*, the better you will understand them.

This translation was made from the French text published by Georges Crès. It first appeared in England, in a limited edition, in 1930. Professor Myron Barker of U.C.L.A. has very kindly helped me to make the work of revision as accurate as possible. Where the reference is so often uncertain, it is hard to avoid some mistakes.

Mr. T. S. Eliot wrote an admirable introduction to the original edition. We have decided not to ask permission to reprint this, however, since it is already available in his *Selected Essays, 1917–1932,* published by Harcourt Brace.

All the illustrations reproduced in this book are by Baudelaire himself. Baudelaire was not only an art-critic of the first rank, he had remarkable artistic talent. Daumier, whose portrait he once drew, said of him that he might have become a great draftsman, if he had not preferred to be a great poet.

The first four drawings are, of course, self-portraits. Next comes a page of sketches for his novel, *La Fanfarlo*. Next, a portrait of Jeanne Duval—the only authenticated one we have. The last two drawings are of unidentified or imaginary women. On the first of these, Baudelaire has written: 'A specimen of Antique Beauty, dedicated

15

to Chenavard.' Chenavard, whose name also appears in the text of the *Intimate Journals*, was a painter and philosopher of the period. Baudelaire evidently intended a caricature of his style.

c. i., *September, 1946*

Charles Baudelaire

INTIMATE
JOURNALS

Squibs

Even though God did not exist, Religion would be none the less holy and divine.

God is the sole being who has no need to exist in order to reign.

That which is created by the Mind is more living than Matter.

Love is the desire to prostitute oneself. There is, indeed, no exalted pleasure which cannot be related to prostitution.

At the play, in the ball-room, each one enjoys possession of all.

What is Art? Prostitution.

The pleasure of being in crowds is a mysterious expression of sensual joy in the multiplication of Number.

All is Number. Number is in all. Number is in the individual. Ecstasy is a Number.

Inclinations to wastefulness ought, when a man is mature, to be replaced by a wish to concentrate and to produce.

Love may spring from a generous sentiment, the de-

21

sire for prostitution; but it is soon corrupted by the desire for ownership.

Love wishes to emerge from itself, to become, like the conqueror with the conquered, a part of its victim, yet to preserve, at the same time, the privileges of the conqueror.

The sensual delights of one who keeps a mistress are at once those of an angel and a landlord. Charity and cruelty. Indeed, they are independent of sex, of beauty and of the animal species.

The green shadows in the moist evenings of summer.

Immense depths of thought in expressions of common speech; holes dug by generations of ants.

The story of the Hunter, concerning the intimate relation between cruelty and love.

II

Squibs. Of the feminine nature of the Church, as a reason for her omnipotence.

Of violet (love repressed, mysterious, veiled; canoness colour).

The priest is a tremendous figure, because he makes the crowd believe marvellous things.

That the Church should wish to do all things and be all things is a law of human nature.

The People adore authority.

Priests are the servants and sectaries of the imagination.
Revolutionary maxim: the throne and the altar.
E. G. or The Seductive Adventuress.
Religious intoxication of the great cities.
Pantheism. I am all things. All things are myself.
Whirlwind.

III

Squibs. I believe I have already set down in my notes
that Love greatly resembles an application of torture or a
surgical operation. But this idea can be developed, and
in the most ironic manner. For even when two lovers love
passionately and are full of mutual desire, one of the two
will always be cooler or less self-abandoned than the other.
He or she is the surgeon or executioner; the other, the
patient or victim. Do you hear these sighs—preludes to a
shameful tragedy—these groans, these screams, these
rattling gasps? Who has not uttered them, who has not
inexorably wrung them forth? What worse sights than
these could you encounter at an inquisition conducted by
adept torturers? These eyes, rolled back like the sleep-
walker's, these limbs whose muscles burst and stiffen as
though subject to the action of a galvanic battery—such
frightful, such curious phenomena are undoubtedly never
obtained from even the most extreme cases of intoxication, of delirium, of opium-taking. The human face,

which Ovid believed fashioned to reflect the stars, speaks here only of an insane ferocity, relaxing into a kind of death. For I should consider it indeed a sacrilege to apply the word "ecstasy" to this species of decomposition.

A terrible pastime, in which one of the players must forfeit possession of himself!

It was once asked, in my hearing, what was the greatest pleasure in Love? Someone, of course, answered: To receive, and someone else: To give oneself— The former said: The pleasure of pride, and the latter: The voluptuousness of humility. All those swine talked like *The Imitation of Jesus Christ*. Finally, there was a shameless Utopian who affirmed that the greatest pleasure in Love was to beget citizens for the State. For my part, I say: the sole and supreme pleasure in Love lies in the absolute knowledge of doing *evil*. And man and woman know, from birth, that in Evil is to be found all voluptuousness.

IV

Schemes. Squibs. Projects. Comedy à la Silvestre. Barbora and the sheep.

Chenavard has created a superhuman type.

My homage to Levaillant.

The Preface, a blend of mysteriousness and drollery.

Dreams and the theory of dreams, in the manner of Swedenborg.

The thought of Campbell (*The conduct of life*).
Concentration.
Power of the fixed idea.
Absolute frankness, the means of originality.
To relate pompously things which are comic. . . .

V

Squibs. Suggestions. When a man takes to his bed, nearly all his friends have a secret desire to see him die; some to prove that his health is inferior to their own, others in the disinterested hope of being able to study a death-agony.

The Arabesque is the most spiritualistic of designs.

VI

Squibs. Suggestions. The man of letters shakes foundations. He promotes the taste for intellectual gymnastics.

The Arabesque is the most ideal of all designs.

We love women in so far as they are strangers to us. To love intelligent women is a pleasure of the pederast. Thus it follows that bestiality excludes pederasty.

The spirit of buffoonery does not necessarily exclude Charity, but this is rare.

Enthusiasm applied to things other than abstractions is a sign of weakness and disease.

Thinness is more naked, more indecent than corpulence.

VII

Tragic Sky. An abstract epithet applied to a material entity.

Man drinks in light with the atmosphere. Thus the masses are right in saying that the night air is unhealthy for work.

The masses are born fire-worshippers.

Fireworks, conflagrations, incendiaries.

If one imagined a born fire-worshipper, a born Parsee, one could write a story . . .

VIII

Mistakes made about people's faces are due to an eclipse of the real image by some hallucination to which it gives rise.

Know therefore the pleasures of an austere life and pray, pray without ceasing. Prayer is the fountain of strength. (*Altar of the Will. Moral dynamic. The Sorcery of the Sacraments. Hygiene of the Soul.*)

Music excavates Heaven.

Jean-Jacques said that he always entered a café with a certain emotional disturbance. For a timid nature, the ticket-office in a theatre is rather like the tribunal of Hell.

Life has but one true charm: the charm of gambling. But what if we are indifferent to gain or loss?

IX

Suggestions. Squibs. Nations—like families—only produce great men in spite of themselves. They make every effort *not* to produce them. And thus the great man has need, if he is to exist, of a power of attack greater than the power of resistance developed by several millions of individuals.

Of sleep, every evening's sinister adventure, it may be observed that men go daily to their beds with an audacity which would be beyond comprehension did we not know that it is the result of their ignorance of danger.

X

There are some skins as hard as tortoise shell against which scorn has no power.

Many friends, many gloves. Those who loved me have been despised persons; worthy of being despised, I might even say, if I were determined to flatter the respectable.

For Girardin to speak Latin! *Pecudesque locutae.*

It was typical of a Society without faith to send Robert Houdin to the Arabs to convert them from belief in miracles.

XI

These great and beautiful ships, imperceptibly poised (swayed) on calm waters; these stout ships, with their out-of-work, home-sick air—are they not saying to us in dumb show: When shall we set sail for happiness?

Do not neglect the marvellous element in drama— the magical and the romanesque.

The surroundings, the atmospheres in which the whole narrative must be steeped. (See *Usher*, and compare this with the most intense sensations of hashish and opium.)

XII

Are there mathematical lunacies and madmen who believe that two and two make three? In other words, can hallucination invade the realms of pure reason—if the words do not cry out (at being joined together)? If, when a man has fallen into habits of idleness, of day-dreaming and of sloth, putting off his most important duties continually till the morrow, another man were to wake him up one morning with heavy blows of a whip and were to whip him unmercifully, until he who was unable to work for pleasure worked now for fear—would not that man, the chastiser, be his benefactor and truest friend? Moreover, one may go so far as to affirm that pleasure itself would follow, and this with much better reason than when it is said: love comes after marriage.

Similarly, in politics, the real saint is he who chastises and massacres the People, for the good of the People.

Tuesday, May 13, 1856

Take some copies to Michel.
Write to Moun,
to Urriès.
to Maria Clemm.
Send to Madame Dumay to know if Mirès . . .
That which is not slightly distorted lacks sensible appeal; from which it follows that irregularity—that is to say, the unexpected, surprise and astonishment, are an essential part and characteristic of beauty.

XIII

Notes. Squibs. Théodore de Banville is not precisely a materialist; he gives forth light.

His poetry represents happy hours.

Whenever you receive a letter from a creditor write fifty lines upon some extra-terrestrial subject, and you will be saved.

A great smile on the beautiful face of a giant.

31

XIV

Of suicide and suicidal mania considered in their bearings upon statistics, medicine, and philosophy.

BRIERE DE BOISMONT

Look up the passage: *To live with someone who feels towards you nothing but aversion. . . .*

The portrait of *Serenus* by Seneca. That of *Stagirus* by St. John Chrysostom. *Acedia,* the malady of Monks.

Taedium Vitae.

XV

Squibs. Translation and paraphrase of *La Passion rapporte tout à elle.*

Spiritual and physical pleasures caused by the storm, electricity and the thunderbolt, tocsin of dark amorous memories, from the distant years.

XVI

Squibs. I have found a definition of the Beautiful, of my own conception of the Beautiful. It is something intense and sad, something a little vague, leaving scope for conjecture. I am ready, if you will, to apply my ideas to a sentient object, to that object, for example, which Society finds the most interesting of all, a woman's face. A beautiful and seductive head, a woman's head, I mean, makes one dream, but in a confused fashion, at once of pleasure and of sadness; conveys an idea of melancholy, of lassitude, even of satiety—a contradictory impression, of an ardour, that is to say, and a desire for life together with a bitterness which flows back upon them as if from a sense of deprivation and hopelessness. Mystery and regret are also characteristics of the Beautiful.

A beautiful male head has no need to convey, to the eyes of a man, at any rate—though perhaps to those of a woman—this impression of voluptuousness which, in a woman's face, is a provocation all the more attractive the more the face is generally melancholy. But this head also will suggest ardours and passions—spiritual longings—ambitions darkly repressed—powers turned to bitterness through lack of employment—traces, sometimes, of a revengeful coldness (for the archetype of the dandy must not be forgotten here), sometimes, also—and this is one of the most interesting characteristics of Beauty—of mystery, and last of all (let me admit the exact point to which I am a modern in my aesthetics) of Unhappiness. I do not pretend that Joy cannot associate with Beauty, but I will maintain that Joy is one of her most vulgar adornments, while Melancholy may be called her illustrious spouse—so much so that I can scarcely conceive (is my brain become a witch's mirror?) a type

33

of Beauty which has nothing to do with Sorrow. In pursuit of—others might say obsessed by—these ideas, it may be supposed that I have difficulty in not concluding from them that the most perfect type of manly beauty is Satan—as Milton saw him.

XVII

Squibs. Auto-Idolatry. Poetic harmony of character. Eurhythmic of the character and the faculties. To preserve all the faculties. To augment all the faculties.

A cult (Magianism, evocatory magic).

The sacrifice and the act of dedication are the supreme formulae and symbols of barter.

Two fundamental literary qualities, supernaturalism and irony. The individual ocular impression, the aspect in which things present themselves to the writer—then the turn of satanic wit. The supernatural comprises the general colour and accent—that is to say, the intensity, sonority, limpidity, vibrancy, depth and reverberation in Space and Time.

There are moments of existence at which Time and Duration are more profound, and the Sense of Being is enormously quickened.

Of magic as applied to the evocation of the great dead, to the restoration and perfection of health.

Inspiration comes always when man wills it, but it does not always depart when he wishes.

Of language and writing, considered as magical operations, evocatory magic.

Of airs in Woman.

The charming airs, those in which beauty consists, are:

The blasé,

The bored,

The empty-headed,

The impudent,

The frigid,

The introspective,

The imperious,

The capricious,

The naughty,

The ailing,

The feline—a blend of childishness, nonchalance and malice.

In certain semi-supernatural conditions of the spirit, the whole depths of life are revealed within the scene— no matter how commonplace—which one has before one's eyes. This becomes its symbol.

As I was crossing the boulevard, hurrying a little to avoid the carriages, my halo was dislodged and fell into the filth of the macadam. Fortunately, I had time to recover it, but a moment later the unhappy thought slipped into my brain that this was an ill omen; and from that instant the idea would not let me alone; it has given me no peace all day.

Of the cult of oneself as a lover—from the point of view of health, hygiene, the toilet, spiritual nobility, eloquence.

Self-purification and anti-humanity

There is, in the act of love, a great resemblance to torture or to a surgical operation.

There is, in prayer, a magical operation. Prayer is one of the great forces of intellectual dynamism. There is, as it were, an electric current.

The rosary is a medium, a vehicle. It is Prayer brought within the reach of all.

Work—a progressive and accumulative force, yielding interest like capital, in the faculties just as much as by its fruits.

Gambling, even when it is conducted scientifically, is an intermittent force and will be overcome, however fruitful it may be, by continuous work, however little.

If a poet demanded from the State the right to have a few bourgeois in his stable, people would be very much astonished, but if a bourgeois asked for some roast poet, people would think it quite natural.

That would not scandalise our wives, our daughters or our sisters.

Presently he asked permission to kiss her leg, and, profiting by the occasion, he kissed that beautiful limb in such a position that her figure was sharply outlined against the setting sun!

"Pussy, kitty, catkin, my cat, my wolf, my little monkey, big monkey, great big serpent, my little melancholy monkey."

Such caprices of language, too often repeated, such excessive use of animal nicknames, testify to a satanic aspect in love. Have not demons the forms of beasts? The camel of Cazotte—camel, devil and woman.

A man goes pistol-shooting, accompanied by his wife. He sets up a doll and says to his wife: "I shall imagine that this is you." He closes his eyes and shatters the doll. Then he says, as he kisses his companion's hand, "Dear angel, let me thank you for my skill!"

When I have inspired universal horror and disgust, I shall have conquered solitude.

This book is not for our wives, our daughters and our sisters. I have little to do with such things.

There are some tortoise-like carapaces against which contempt ceases to be a pleasure.

Many friends, many gloves—for fear of the itch.

Those who have loved me were despised people, I might even say worthy of being despised, if I were determined to flatter the *respectable*.

God is a scandal—a scandal which pays.

XVIII

Squibs. Despise the sensibility of nobody. Each man's sensibility is his genius.

There are only two places where one pays for the right to spend: women and public latrines.

From a passionate concubinage one may guess at the joys of a young married couple.

The precocious taste for women. I used to confuse the smell of women with the smell of furs. I remember . . . Indeed, I loved my mother for her elegance. I was a precocious dandy.

My ancestors, idiots or maniacs, in their solemn houses, all victims of terrible passions.

The protestant countries lack two elements indispensable to the happiness of a well-bred man; gallantry and devotion.

The mixture of the grotesque and the tragic is agreeable to the spirit, as are discords to the jaded ear.

What is exhilarating in bad taste is the aristocratic pleasure of giving offence.

Germany expresses her dreams by means of line, England by means of perspective.

There is, in the creation of all sublime thought, a nervous concussion which can be felt in the cerebellum.

Spain brings to religion the natural ferocity of Love.

STYLE. The eternal touch, eternal and cosmopolite. Chateaubriand, Alph. Rabbe, Edgar Poe.

XIX

Squibs. Suggestions. It is easy to guess why the rabble dislike cats. A cat is beautiful; it suggests ideas of luxury, cleanliness, voluptuous pleasures . . . etc.

XX

Squibs. A small amount of work, repeated three hundred and sixty-five times, gives three hundred and sixty-five times a small sum of money—that is to say, an enormous sum. *At the same time, glory is achieved. [In the margin] Similarly, a crowd of small pleasures compose happiness.*

To write a pot-boiler, that is genius. I ought to write a pot-boiler.

A really clever remark is a masterpiece.

The tone of Alphonse Rabbe.

39

The tone of a kept woman (*My beautifullest! Oh, you fickle sex!*)

The eternal tone.

The colouring crude, the design profoundly simplified. *The prima donna and the butcher boy.*

My mother is fantastic; one must fear and propitiate her.

Hildebrand the arrogant.

Caesarism of Napoleon III (Letter to Edgar Ney), Pope and Emperor.

XXI

Squibs. Suggestions. To give oneself to Satan. What does this mean?

What can be more absurd than Progress, since man, as the event of each day proves, is for ever the double and equal of man—is for ever, that is to say, in the state of primitive nature! What perils have the forest and the prairie to compare with the daily shocks and conflicts of civilization? Whether man ensnares his dupe upon the boulevard or pierces his victim within the trackless forests, is he not everlasting man, the most perfect of the beasts of prey?

People tell me that I am thirty, but if I have lived three minutes in one . . . am I not ninety years old?

Is not work the salt which preserves mummified souls?

At the beginning of a story attack the subject, no matter where, and open with some very beautiful phrases which will arouse the desire to complete it.

XXII

I believe that the infinite and mysterious charm which lies in the contemplation of a ship, especially of a ship in motion, depends firstly upon its order and symmetry—primal needs of the human spirit as great as those of intricacy and harmony—and, secondly, upon the successive multiplication and generation of all the curves and imaginary figures described in space by the real elements of the object.

The poetic idea which emerges from this operation of line in motion is an hypothesis of an immeasurably vast, complex, yet perfectly harmonised entity, of an animal being possessed of a spirit, suffering all human ambition and sighing all the sighs of men.

You civilised peoples, who are for ever speaking foolishly about *Savages* and *Barbarians*—soon, as d'Aurevilly says, you will have become too worthless *even to be idolators*.

Stoicism, a religion which has but one sacrament: suicide!

To conceive a sketch for a lyrical or fairy extravagance for a pantomime and to translate it into a serious romance.

To plunge the whole into a supernatural, dreamlike atmosphere—the atmosphere of the *great days*. That there should be something lulling, even serene, in passion. Regions of pure poetry.

Moved by contact with those pleasures which were themselves like memories, softened by the thought of a past ill spent, of so many faults, so many quarrels, of so many things which each must hide from the other, he began to weep; and his tears fell warm, in the darkness, upon the bare shoulder of his beloved and still charming mistress. She trembled. She, also, felt moved and softened. The darkness shielded her vanity, her elegant affectation of coldness. These two fallen creatures, who could still suffer, since a vestige of nobility remained with them, embraced impulsively, mingling, in the rain of their tears and kisses, regrets for the past with hopes, all too uncertain, for the future. Never, perhaps, for them, as upon that night of melancholy and forgiveness, had pleasure been so sweet—a pleasure steeped in sorrow and remorse.

Through the night's blackness, he had looked behind him into the depths of the years, then he had thrown himself into the arms of his guilty lover, to recover there the pardon he was granting her.

Hugo often thinks of Prometheus. He applies an

imaginary vulture to his breast, which is seared only by the moxas of vanity. Then, as the hallucination becomes more complex and varied, following always, however, the progressive stages which medical men describe, he believes that a *fiat* of Providence has substituted Jersey for St. Helena.

This man is so little of a poet, so little spiritual, that he would disgust even a solicitor.

Hugo, like a priest, always has his head bowed—bowed so low that he can see nothing except his own navel.

What is not a priesthood nowadays? Youth itself is a priesthood—according to the young.

And what is not a prayer? To sh——— is a prayer—according to the rabble, when they sh———

M. de Pontmartin—a man who has always the air of having just arrived from the provinces.

Man—all mankind, that is to say—is so *naturally* depraved that he suffers less from universal degradation than from the establishment of a reasonable hierarchy.

The world is about to end. Its sole reason for continuance is that it exists. And how feeble is this reason, compared with those which announce the contrary, particularly the following: What, under Heaven, has this world henceforth to do? Even supposing that it continued materially to exist, would this existence be worthy of the

name or the Historical Dictionary? I do not say that the
world will be reduced to the clownish shifts and disorders
of a South American republic, or even that we shall perhaps return to a state of nature and roam the grassy ruins
of our civilization, gun in hand, seeking our food. No;
for these adventures would require a certain remnant of
vital energy, echo of earlier ages. As a new example, as
fresh victims of the inexorable moral laws, we shall perish
by that which we have believed to be our means of existence. So far will machinery have Americanized us, so far
will Progress have atrophied in us all that is spiritual, that
no dream of the Utopians, however bloody, sacrilegious
or unnatural, will be comparable to the result. I appeal to
every thinking man to show me what remains of Life. As
for religion, I believe it useless to speak of it or to search
for its relics, since to give oneself the trouble of denying
God is the sole disgrace in these matters. Ownership
virtually disappeared with the suppression of the rights
of the eldest son; but the time will come when humanity,
like an avenging ogre, will tear their last morsel from
those who believe themselves to be the legitimate heirs of
revolution. And even that will not be the worst.

Human imagination can conceive, without undue difficulty, of republics or other communal states worthy of
a certain glory, if they are directed by holy men, by certain aristocrats. It is not, however, specifically in political

institutions that the universal ruin, or the universal progress—for the name matters little—will be manifested. That will appear in the degradation of the human heart. Need I describe how the last vestiges of statesmanship will struggle painfully in the clutches of universal bestiality, how the governors will be forced—in maintaining themselves and erecting a phantom of order—to resort to measures which would make our men of today shudder, hardened as they are? Then the son will run away from the family not at eighteen but at twelve, emancipated by his gluttonous precocity; he will fly, not to seek heroic adventures, not to deliver a beautiful prisoner from a tower, not to immortalize a garret with sublime thoughts, but to found a business, to enrich himself and to compete with his infamous papa, to be founder and shareholder of a journal which will spread enlightenment and cause *Le Siècle* of that time to be considered as an instrument of superstition. Then the erring, the déclassées, those women who have had several lovers and who are sometimes called Angels, by virtue of and in gratitude for the empty-headed frivolity which illumines, with its fortuitous light, their existences logical as evil—then these women, I say, will be nothing but a pitiless wisdom, a wisdom which condemns everything except money, everything, even the *crimes of the senses*. Then, any shadow of virtue, everything indeed which is not worship of Plutus, will be brought into utter ridicule. Justice, if, at that fortunate epoch, Justice can still exist, will deprive of their civil rights those citizens who are unable to make a fortune. Thy spouse, O bourgeois! Thy chaste better half, whose legitimacy seems to thee poetic—making legality to be henceforth a baseness beneath reproach— vigilant and loving guardian of thy strong-box, will be no more than the absolute type of the kept woman. Thy daughter, with an infantile wantonness, will dream in her cradle that she sells herself for a million—and thou, thyself, O bourgeois—less of a poet even than thou art to-day—thou wilt find no fault in that, thou wilt regret nothing. For there are some qualities in a man which grow strong and prosper only as others diminish and grow less; thanks to the progress of that age, of thy bowels of compassion nothing will remain but the guts!— That age is perhaps very near; who knows if it is not already come and if the coarseness of our perceptions is not the sole obstacle which prevents us from appreciating the nature of the atmosphere in which we breathe?

For myself, who feel within me sometimes the absurdity of a prophet, I know that I shall never achieve the charity of a physician. Lost in this vile world, elbowed by the crowd, I am like a worn-out man, whose eyes see, in the depths of the years behind him, only disillusionment and bitterness, ahead only a tumult in which there is nothing new, whether of enlightenment or of suffering. In the evening, when this man has filched from his destiny a few hours of pleasure, when he is lulled by the process of digestion, forgetful—as far as possible—of the past, content with the present and resigned to the future, exhilarated by his own nonchalance and dandyism, proud that he is less base than the passers-by, he says to himself, as he contemplates the smoke of his cigar: What does it matter to me what becomes of these perceptions?

I believe I have wandered into what those of the trade call a hors-d'oeuvre. Nevertheless, I will let these pages stand—since I wish to record my days of anger.

My Heart Laid Bare

XXIII

Of the vaporization and centralization of the *Ego*. Everything depends on that.

Of a certain sensual pleasure in the company of those who behave extravagantly.

(I intend to begin *My Heart laid bare,* no matter where or how, and to continue it from day to day, following the inspiration of the day and the circumstances, provided that the inspiration is vital.)

XXIV

Anyone, provided that he can be amusing, has the right to talk of himself.

XXV

I understand how one can desert a cause in order to experience the sensation of serving another.

It would perhaps be pleasant to be alternately victim and executioner.

XXVI

Stupidities of Girardin:

"We are accustomed to take the bull by the horns. Let us therefore take the speech by its conclusion" (November 7, 1861).

Then Girardin believes that the horns of bulls are set in their behinds. He confounds the horns with the tail.

*"Before imitating the Ptolemies of French journalism, the Belgian journalists have taken the trouble to meditate upon the problem which I have been studying for the last thirty years in all its aspects—as the volume which will shortly appear, entitled 'Questions de presse,' will prove—with the result that they are in no hurry to treat as a matter for superlative ridicule * an opinion which is as indisputable as the statement that the earth revolves and that the sun does not revolve."*

EMILE DE GIRARDIN

---

* There are those who pretend to have no difficulty in believing that the earth turns upon its own axis, the sky remaining stationary. These persons do not perceive that, when all which takes place around us is considered, their opinion is a matter for *superlative ridicule* (πανυ γελοίοτατον). Ptolemy (*Almagest.*, Book I, Chapter VI).

Et habet mea mentrita mentum.

GIRARDIN.

XXVII

Woman is the opposite of the Dandy. Therefore she should inspire horror.

Woman is hungry, and she wants to eat; thirsty, and she wants to drink.

She is in rut and she wants to be possessed.

What admirable qualities!

Woman is *natural,* that is to say abominable.

Thus she is always vulgar; the opposite, in fact, of the Dandy.

Concerning the Legion of Honour. The man who solicits the Cross has the air of saying: If I am not decorated for having done my duty, I shall cease to do it.

If a man has merit, what is the good of decorating him? If he has none, he can be decorated, since it will give him distinction.

To consent to being decorated is to recognize that the State or a prince has the right to judge of your merits, to dignify you, etc. . . .

Besides, Christian humility forbids the Cross, even if pride does not.

Calculation in favour of God. Nothing exists without purpose.

Therefore my existence has a purpose.

What purpose? I do not know.

Therefore, it is not I who have appointed that purpose. It is someone wiser than I.

It is therefore necessary to pray to this someone to enlighten me. That is the wisest course.

The Dandy should aspire to be uninterruptedly sublime. He should live and sleep in front of a mirror.

XXVIII

Analysis of the counter-religions. Example: sacred prostitution.

What is sacred prostitution?

Nervous excitement.

The mystery of Paganism. Mysticism: the common feature of Paganism and Christianity.

Paganism and Christianity confirm each other.

The Revolution and the Cult of Reason confirm the doctrine of Sacrifice.

Superstition is the well of all truths.

XXIX

There is in all Change something at once sordid and agreeable, which smacks of infidelity and household removals. This is sufficient to explain the French Revolution.

XXX

My wild excitement in 1848.

What was the nature of that excitement?

The taste for revenge. Natural pleasure in destruction. Literary excitement; memories of my reading.

The 15th of May. Still the pleasure in destruction. A legitimate pleasure, if what is natural be legitimate.

The horrors of June. Madness of the People and madness of the Bourgeoisie. Natural delight in crime.

My fury at the Coup d'Etat. How many gunshots have I endured! Another Bonaparte! What infamy!

And, meanwhile, all is quiet. Has not the President some right to invoke?

What Napoleon III is. What he is worth. To find the explanation of his nature and of his mission under Providence.

XXXI

To be a useful person has always appeared to me something particularly horrible.

1848 was amusing only because of those castles in the air which each man built for his Utopia.

1848 was charming only through an excess of the ridiculous.

Robespierre can only be admired because he has made several beautiful phrases.

XXXII

Revolution confirms Superstition, by offering sacrifice.

XXXIII

Politics. I have no convictions, as men of my century understand the word, because I have no ambition. There is no basis in me for a conviction.

There is a certain cowardice, a certain weakness, rather, among respectable folk.

Only brigands are convinced—of what? That they must succeed. And so they do succeed.

How should I succeed, since I have not even the desire to make the attempt?

Glorious empires may be founded upon crime and noble religions upon imposture.

Nevertheless, I have some convictions, in a higher sense, which could not be understood by the people of my time.

XXXIV

The sense of *solitude,* since my childhood. In spite of my family, above all when surrounded by my comrades —the sense of a destiny eternally solitary.

Yet a taste for life and for pleasure which is very keen.

XXXV

Nearly our whole lives are employed in foolish en-
quiries. Nevertheless, there are questions which should
excite man's curiosity in the highest degree, and which,
to judge from his customary mode of life, do not inspire
him with any.

Where are our dead friends?

Why are we here?

Do we come from some other place?

What is free will?

Can it be reconciled with the laws of Providence?

Is there a finite or an infinite number of souls?

What of the number of habitable lands? Etc., etc. . . .

XXXVI

Nations only produce great men in spite of themselves.
Thus the great man is the conqueror of his whole nation.

The ridiculous modern comic religions:

Molière.

Béranger.

Garibaldi.

XXXVII

Belief in Progress is a doctrine of idlers and Belgians.
It is the individual relying upon his neighbours to do his
work.

There cannot be any Progress (true progress, that is to say, moral) except within the individual and by the individual himself.

But the world is composed of people who can think only in common, in the herd. Like the *Sociétés belges*.

There are also people who can only take their pleasures in a flock. The true hero takes his pleasure alone.

XXXVIII

Eternal superiority of the Dandy.

What is the Dandy?

XXXIX

My views on the theatre. In childhood and still to-day, the thing which I have always thought most beautiful about the theatre is the chandelier—a fine, luminous, crystalline object with a complex spherical symmetry.

Meanwhile, I do not entirely deny the value of dramatic literature. Only I should like the actors mounted on very high pattens, wearing masks more expressive than the human face and speaking through megaphones; also the female parts should be played by men.

But, after all, whether seen through the big or the little end of the opera glass, the chandelier has always appeared to me to be the protagonist.

XL

One must work, if not from inclination at least from despair, since, as I have fully proved, to work is less wearisome than to amuse oneself.

XLI

There are in every man, always, two simultaneous allegiances, one to God, the other to Satan.

Invocation of God, or Spirituality, is a desire to climb higher; that of Satan, or animality, is delight in descent. It is to this last that love for woman and intimate conversations with animals, dogs, cats, etc. . . . must be ascribed. The joys which derive from these two loves are appropriate to the nature of these two loves.

XLII

Intoxication of humanity: a great picture to paint:
From the aspect of Charity.
From the aspect of licentiousness.
From the aspect of literature or of the actor.

XLIII

The Question (torture), when considered as the art of discovering the truth, is a barbarous stupidity; it is the application of a material means to a spiritual end.

The penalty of death is the expression of a mystical idea, totally misunderstod to-day. The penalty of death does not attempt to *save* Society, that is, in the material sense. It attempts to save *spiritually* Society and the guilty person. That the sacrifice may be perfect there should be joy and consent on the part of the victim. To give chloroform to a person condemned to death would be impious, for he would thereby be deprived of his consciousness of grandeur as a victim and of his hopes of attaining Paradise.

As for torture, it has been devised by the evil half of man's nature, which is thirsty for voluptuous pleasures. Cruelty and sensual pleasure are identical, like extreme heat and extreme cold.

XLIV

My opinion of the vote and of the right of election. Of the rights of man.

The element of baseness in any sort of government employment.

A Dandy does nothing. Can you imagine a dandy addressing the common herd, except to make game of them?

There is no form of rational and assured government save an aristocracy.

A monarchy or a republic, based upon democracy, are equally absurd and feeble.

The immense nausea of advertisements.

There are but three beings worthy of respect: the priest, the warrior and the poet. To know, to kill and to create.

The rest of mankind may be taxed and drudged, they are born for the stable, that is to say, to practise what they call *professions*.

XLV

We should observe that the abolishers of the death penalty must be more or less *interested* in its abolition.

Often they are guillotiners. Their attitude may be thus expressed: "I want to be able to cut off your head, but you shan't touch mine."

The abolishers of the Soul (*materialists*) are necessarily abolishers of *hell;* they, certainly, are *interested*.

At all events, they are people who *fear to live again*— lazy people.

XLVI

Madame de Metternich, although she is a princess, has forgotten to answer me, regarding what I said about her and Wagner.

Nineteenth-century manners.

XLVII

The story of my translation of Edgar Poe.

The story of the *Fleurs du Mal*. The humiliation of being misunderstood and my lawsuit.

The story of my relations with all the celebrated men of the age.

Some amusing portraits of certain imbeciles:

Clément de Ris.

Castagnary.

Portraits of magistrates, officials, newspaper editors, etc.

Portraits of artists in general.

Of the chief editor and of the rank and file. The immense pleasure which the French people take in being regimented. It is the *If I were King!*

Portraits and Anecdotes.

François Buloz—Houssaye—the precious Rouy—de Calonne—Charpentier, who corrects his authors, by virtue of the equality bestowed on all men by the immortal principles of (17)89—Chevalier, a really typical editor-in-chief under the Empire.

XLVIII

On George Sand. The woman Sand is the Prudhomme of immorality.

She has always been a moralist.

Only she used to work as an anti-moralist.

She has never been an artist. She has that celebrated *flowing style,* so dear to the bourgeois.

She is stupid, she is clumsy, and she is a chatterbox. She has, in her moral concepts, the same profundity of judgment and delicacy of feeling as a concierge or a kept woman.

What she says about her mother.

What she says about Poetry.

Her love for the working classes.

It is indeed a proof of the degradation of the men of this century that several have been capable of falling in love with this latrine.

See the preface to *Mademoiselle La Quintinie,* in which she pretends that true Christians do not believe in Hell.

Sand represents the *God of decent folk,* the god of concierges and thieving servants.

She has good reasons for wishing to abolish Hell.

XLIX

The Devil and George Sand. It must not be supposed that the Devil only tempts men of genius. Doubtless, he despises imbeciles, but he does not disdain their cooperation. Quite the reverse; it is upon them that he builds his greatest hopes.

Consider George Sand. She is, first and last, a *prodigious blockhead*, but she is *possessed*. It is the Devil who has persuaded her to trust in her *good-nature* and *common-sense,* that she may persuade all other prodigious blockheads to trust in their good-nature and common-sense.

I cannot think of this stupid creature without a certain shudder of horror. If I were to meet her, I should not be able to resist throwing a stoup of holy water at her head.

L

George Sand is one of those decayed *ingénues* who will never leave the boards. I have lately read a preface (the preface to *Mademoiselle La Quintinie*) in which she pretends that the true Christian cannot believe in Hell. She has good reasons for wishing to abolish Hell.

LI

I am sick of France; chiefly because everybody is like Voltaire.

Emerson has forgotten Voltaire in his *Representative Men*. He could have written a fine chapter entitled *Voltaire, or the Anti-Poet,* the king of loungers, the prince of triflers, the anti-artist, the preacher to concierges, the Father Gigogne of the Editors of *Le Siècle*.

LII

In *Les Oreilles du Comte de Chesterfield*, Voltaire jests about our immortal soul, which has dwelt for nine months amidst excrement and urine. Voltaire, like all loafers, hates mystery.

Being unable to abolish Love, the Church has desired at least to disinfect it, and has invented marriage.

Note.—He might, at least, have traced, in this localisation, a malicious and satirical intent of Providence against Love, and, in the mode of generation, a symbol of original sin, since we can only make love with our excretory organs.

LIII

Portrait of the literary rabble.

Doctor Estaminetus Crapulosus Pedantissimus. His portrait executed in the manner of Praxiteles.

His pipe.

His opinions.

His Hegelism.

His foulness.

His ideas on art.

His spleen.

His jealousy.

A fine portrait of modern youth.

LIV

Φαρμαχοτρίδης, ἀνὴρ καὶ τῶν τούς ὄφεις ἐς τα δαυματα τρεφοντων.

AELIAN (?)

LV

Theology. What is the Fall?
If it is unity become duality, it is God who has fallen.
In other words, would not creation be the fall of God?
Dandyism. What is the superior man?
He is not a specialist.
He is a man of leisure and of liberal education.
To be rich and to love work.

LVI

Why does the man of parts prefer harlots to Society women, although they are equally stupid?
To discover this.

LVII

There are certain women who are like the red ribbon of the Legion of Honour. They are no longer desired because they have been contaminated by certain men.

It is for the same reason that I would not put on the breeches of a man with the itch.

What is annoying about Love is that it is a crime in which one cannot do without an accomplice.

LVIII

Study of the great malady, horror of one's home. Causes of the malady. Progressive growth of the malady.

Indignation aroused by the universal fatuity of all classes, all persons, of both sexes, at all ages.

Man loves man so much that, even when he flees from the town, he is still in search of the mob; he wishes, in fact, to rebuild the town in the country.

LIX

Lecture by Durandeau on the Japanese. ("I am, before all else, a Frenchman.") The Japanese are monkeys, Darjon it was who told me so.

Lecture by a doctor, a friend of Mathieu, on the art of not having children, Moses, and the immortality of the Soul. Art is a civilizing influence (Castagnary).

LX

The faces of a sage man and his family, who live on the sixth floor, drinking *café au lait*.

Lord Nacquart senior and Lord Nacquart junior.

How the Nacquart son has come to be a counsel in the Court of Appeal.

LXI

Of the delight in and preference for military metaphors shown by the French. Here every metaphor wears moustaches.

Militant literature.

To hold the breach.

To keep the flag flying.

To emerge with flying colours.

To plunge into the fray.

One of the old brigade.

All these glorious phrases are commonly applied to drunkards and bar-flies.

LXII

French metaphors.

A soldier of the judicial press (Bertin).

The militant press.

LXIII

To be added to the military metaphors:

The fighting poets.

The literary vanguard.

This use of military metaphor reveals minds not militant but formed for discipline, that is, for compliance;

minds born servile, Belgian minds, which can think only collectively.

LXIV

Desire for Pleasure attaches us to the Present. Care for our safety makes us dependent upon the Future.

He who clings to Pleasure, that is, to the Present, makes me think of a man rolling down a slope who, in trying to grasp hold of some bushes, tears them up and carries them with him in his fall.

To be, *before all else, a great man* and a *saint* according to one's own standards.

LXV

Of the People's hatred of Beauty. Examples: Jeanne and Mme. Muller.

LXVI

Political. After all, the supreme glory of Napoleon III, in the eyes of History and of the French people, will have been to prove that anybody can govern a great nation as soon as they have got control of the telegraph and the national press.

They are imbeciles who believe that such things can be accomplished without the permission of the People— and that glory can only be founded upon virtue!

Dictators are the servants of the People—nothing more; a damnable job, the glory and the result of adapting a brain to the requirements of the national idiocy.

LXVII

What is Love?
The need to emerge from oneself.
Man is an animal which adores.
To adore is to sacrifice and prostitute oneself.
Thus all Love is prostitution.

LXVIII

The most prostitute of all beings is the Supreme Being, God Himself, since for each man he is the friend above all others; since he is the common, inexhaustible fount of Love.

PRAYER

Do not punish me through my Mother and do not punish my Mother on my behalf—I entrust to your keeping the souls of my father and of Mariette— Give me the strength immediately to perform my daily task and thus to become a hero and a saint.

LXIX

A chapter on the indestructible, eternal, universal, and ingenious ferocity of Men.

Of delight in bloodshed.

Of the intoxication of bloodshed.

Of the intoxication of the mob.

Of the intoxication of the tortured (Damiens).

LXX

There are no great men save the poet, the priest, and the soldier.

The man who sings, the man who offers up sacrifice, and the man who sacrifices himself.

The rest are born for the whip.

Let us beware of the rabble, of common-sense, good-nature, inspiration, and evidence.

LXXI

I have always been astonished that women are allowed to enter churches. What conversation can they have with God?

The Eternal Venus (capricious, hysterical, full of whims) is one of the seductive shapes of the Devil.

On the day when a young writer corrects his first proof-sheet he is as proud as a schoolboy who has just got his first dose of pox.

Do not forget a long chapter on the art of divination by water, by the cards, by chiromancy, etc.

LXXII

Woman cannot distinguish between her soul and her body. She simplifies things, like an animal. A cynic would say that it is because she has nothing but a body.

A chapter on *The Toilet*.

Morality of the toilet, the delights of the toilet.

LXXIII

Of nincompoops.

Of professors.

Of judges.

Of priests.

And of Cabinet Ministers.

The precious little great men of the day.

Renan.

Feydeau.

Octave Feuillet.

Scholl.

The editors of newspapers, Francois Buloz, Houssaye, Rouy, Girardin, Texier, de Calonne, Solar, Turgan, Dalloz.

A list of gutternsipes. Solar first of all.

LXXIV

To be a great man and a saint by *one's own standards*, that is all that matters.

La Fanfarlo

LXXV

Nadar is the most astounding example of vitality. Adrien used to tell me that this brother Felix had all his viscera double. I have been jealous of him, seeing him succeed so well in everything which is not abstract.

Veuillot is so uncouth and such an enemy of the arts that one might suppose the whole democracy of the world had taken refuge in his breast.

Development of the portrait. Supremacy of the pure idea over the Christian and the *babouviste* communist.

The fanaticism of humility. Not even to aspire to understand religion.

LXXVI

Music.

Of slavery.

Of Society women.

Of prostitutes.

Of magistrates.

Of the sacraments.

The man of letters is the enemy of the world.

Of bureaucrats.

LXXVII

In Love, as in nearly all human affairs, a satisfactory relationship is the result of a misunderstanding. This misunderstanding constitutes pleasure. The man cries: Oh, my angel. The woman coos: Mamma! Mamma! And these two imbeciles are persuaded that they think alike. The unbridgeable gulf—the cause of their failure in communication remains—unbridged.

LXXVIII

Why is the spectacle of the sea so infinitely and eternally agreeable?

Because the sea presents at once the idea of immensity and of movement. Six or seven leagues represent for man the radius of the infinite. An infinite in little. What matter, if it suffices to suggest the idea of all infinity? Twelve or fourteen leagues of liquid in movement are enough to convey to man the highest expression of beauty which he can encounter in his transient abode.

LXXIX

Nothing upon the earth is interesting except religions. What is the universal religion? (Chateaubriand, de Maistre, the Alexandrines, Capé.)

There is a universal religion devised for the alchemists of thought, a religion which has nothing to do with Man, considered as a divine memento.

LXXX

Saint-Marc Girardin has uttered one phrase which will endure: *"Let us be mediocre!"*

Let us put this beside the words of Robespierre: "Those who do not believe in the immortality of their being pass judgment upon themselves."

This phrase of Saint-Marc Girardin implies an immense hatred of the sublime.

Whoever sees Saint-Marc Girardin walking in the street is reminded immediately of a fat goose, full of self-conceit, but bewildered and waddling along the high road in front of the stage-coach.

LXXXI

Theory of the true civilization. It is not to be found in gas or steam or table-turning. It consists in the diminution of the traces of original sin.

Nomad peoples, shepherds, hunters, farmers and even cannibals, may all, by virtue of energy and personal dignity, be the superiors of our races of the West.

These will perhaps be destroyed.

Theocracy and communism.

LXXXII

I have grown, for the most part, by means of leisure. To my great detriment; for leisure without fortune breeds debts and the insults which result from debts.

But to my great profit also, so far as sensibility is concerned and meditation and the faculty of dandyism and dilletantism.

Other men of letters are, for the most part, common, ignorant earth-grubbers.

LXXXIII

The modern girl according to the publishers.

The modern girl according to the editors-in-chief.

The modern girl as a bugbear, a monster, an assassin of art.

The modern girl as she is in reality.

A little blockhead and a little slut. The extreme of imbecility combined with the extreme of depravity.

There are in the modern girl all the despicable qualities of the footpad and the schoolboy.

LXXXIV

Warning to non-communists:
All is common property, even God.

LXXXV

The Frenchman is a farmyard animal, so well domesticated that he dares not jump over any fence. Witness his tastes in art and literature.

He is an animal of the Latin race; he does not object to filth in his place of abode; and in literature he is scatophagous. He dotes on excrements. That is what pothouse men of letters call the *Gallic salt.*

A choice example of French depravity: of the nation which pretends to be independent above all others.

(Here a paragraph cut out from a newspaper is fastened to the manuscript.)

The following extract from M. de Vaulabelle's fine book will suffice to give an idea of the impression made by Lavalette's escape upon the least enlightened section of the Royalist party:

"The tide of Royalism, at this period of the Second Restoration, was rising almost to the point of madness. The young Josephine de Lavalette was receiving her education at one of the principal convents of Paris (l'Abbaye-au-Bois). She had left it merely to come to kiss her father. When she returned after the escape, and when the very modest part she had played in it was known, an immense outcry was raised against the child; the nuns and her companions avoided her and a number of the parents declared that they would remove their daughters if she were allowed to remain there. They did not wish, they said, to allow their daughters to come into contact with a young person who had been guilty of such conduct and such an example. When Madame de Lavalette recovered her liberty, six weeks later, she was obliged to take away her daughter."

LXXXVI

Princes and generations. It is equally unjust to attribute to reigning princes the merits or the vices of those whom they actually govern.

These merits and these vices are almost always, as statistics and logic can prove, attributable to the influence of the preceding government. Louis XIV inherits from the men of Louis XIII: glory. Napoleon I inherits from the men of the Republic: glory. Louis-Philippe inherits from the men of Charles X: glory. Napoleon inherits from the men of Louis-Philippe: dishonour.

It is always the preceding government which is responsible for the morals of its successor, in so far as a government can be responsible for anything.

The sudden cutting short of a reign by circumstance prevents this law from being quite exact as regards time. One cannot mark exactly where an influence ends, but this influence will survive throughout the whole generation which has undergone it in youth.

LXXXVII

Of youth's hatred of the quoters of precedents. The quoter is its enemy.

"Even spelling I would hand over to the hangman."
THÉOPHILE GAUTIER.

A fine picture to paint: the literary riff-raff.

Not to forget a portrait of Forgues, the plagiarist, the cream-skinner of letters.

Ineradicable desire for prostitution in the heart of man, whence is born his horror of solitude. He wants to be *two*. The man of genius wants to be *one,* and therefore solitary. Glory is to remain *one,* and to prostitute oneself in an individual manner.

It is this horror of solitude, this need to lose his *ego* in exterior flesh, which man calls grandly *the need for love.*

Two fine religions, immortalized upon walls, the eternal obsessions of the People: a p——— (the antique phallus) and "Long live Barbès!" or "Down with Philippe!" or "Long live the Republic!"

LXXXVIII

To study in all its modes, in the works of nature and in the works of man, the universal and eternal law of gradation, of the *little by little,* of the *by degrees,* with forces progressively increasing, like compound interest in money matters.

It is the same with *literary and artistic talents;* it is the same with the variable treasures of the *will.*

LXXXIX

The crush of minor literary men whom one sees at funerals, distributing handshakes and trying to catch the eye of the writer of the *obituary notice.*

Of the funerals of famous men.

XC

Molière. My opinion of *Tartuffe* is that it is not a comedy but a pamphlet. An atheist, if he is simply a well-educated man, would reflect, in thinking about this piece, that there are certain serious questions which must never be referred to the rabble.

XCI

To glorify the cult of pictures (my great, my unique, my primitive passion).

To glorify vagabondage and what may be called bohemianism. Cult of the multiple sensations expressed by music. Refer here to Liszt.

Of the necessity of thrashing women.

One can chastise those whom one loves. As in the case of children. But that implies the sorrow of despising those whom one loves.

Of cuckolds and cuckoldom.

The sorrows of the cuckold.

They are born of his pride, of false reasoning concerning honour and happiness, and of a love which has been foolishly withdrawn from God to be bestowed upon his fellow-creatures. It is always the animal idolator being deceived in his idol.

XCII

Analysis of insolent imbecility. Clément de Ris and Paul Pérignon.

XCIII

The more a man cultivates the arts the less he fornicates. A more and more apparent cleavage occurs between the spirit and the brute.

Only the brute is really potent. Sexuality is the lyricism of the masses.

To fornicate is to aspire to enter into another; the artist never emerges from himself.

I have forgotten the name of that slut. Bah! I shall remember it at the last judgment.

Music conveys the idea of space.

So do all the arts, more or less; since they are *number* and since number is a translation of space.

To will every day to be the greatest of men!

XCIV

When I was a child I wanted sometimes to be pope, but a military pope, and sometimes to be an actor.

The pleasures that I derived from these two phantasies.

XCV

Even when quite a child I felt two conflicting sensations in my heart: the horror of life and the ecstasy of life. That, indeed, was the mark of a neurasthenic idler.

XCVI

Nations produce great men only in spite of themselves.

Speaking of the actor and of my childish dreams, a chapter upon what constitutes, in the human soul, the vocation of the actor, the glory of the actor, the art of the actor and his situation in the world.

The theory of Legouvé. Is Legouvé a dispassionate joker, a Swift, who has tried to make France swallow a new absurdity?

His choice. Good, in the sense that Samson is not an actor.

Of the true grandeur of pariahs.

It is possible, indeed, that virtue would injure the talents of pariahs.

XCVII

Commerce is, in its very essence, *satanic*. Commerce is return of the loan, a loan in which there is the understanding: *give me more than I give you.*

The spirit of every business-man is completely depraved.

Commerce is *natural,* therefore *shameful.*

The least vile of all merchants is he who says: "Let us be virtuous, since, thus, we shall gain much more money than the fools who are dishonest."

For the merchant, even honesty is a financial speculation.

Commerce is satanic, because it is the basest and vilest form of egoism.

XCVIII

When Jesus Christ says, "Blessed are they that hunger, for they shall be filled," Jesus Christ is calculating on probabilities.

XCIX

The world only goes round by misunderstanding.

It is by universal misunderstanding that all agree.

For if, by ill luck, people understood each other, they would never agree.

The man of intelligence, who will never agree with anyone, should cultivate a pleasure in the conversation of imbeciles and the study of worthless books. From these he will derive a sardonic amusement which will largely repay him for his pains.

C

Any official, whether a minister, a theatre manager or a newspaper editor, can sometimes be an estimable individual, but he is never a man of distinction. They are persons without personality, unoriginal, born for office, that is, for domestic service to the public.

CI

God and His profundity. It is possible even for the intelligent man to seek in God that helper and friend whom he can never find. God is the eternal confidant in that tragedy of which each man is hero. Perhaps there are usurers and assassins who say to God: "Lord, grant that my next enterprise may be successful!" But the prayers of these vile persons do not mar the virtue and joy of my own.

CII

Every idea is endowed of itself with immortal life, like a human being. All created form, even that which is created by man, is immortal. For form is independent of matter: molecules do not constitute form.

Anecdotes of Emile Douay and Constantin Guys, and how they destroyed, or believed that they destroyed, their works.

CIII

It is impossible to glance through any newspaper, no matter what the day, the month or the year, without finding on every line the most frightful traces of human perversity, together with the most astonishing boasts of probity, charity, and benevolence and the most brazen statements regarding the progress of civilization.

Every journal, from the first line to the last, is nothing but a tissue of horrors. Wars, crimes, thefts, lecheries, tortures, the evil deeds of princes, of nations, of private individuals; an orgy of universal atrocity.

And it is with this loathsome appetizer that civilized man daily washes down his morning repast. Everything in this world oozes crime: the newspaper, the street wall, and the human countenance.

I am unable to comprehend how a man of honor could take a newspaper in his hands without a shudder of disgust.

CIV

The power of the amulet as displayed by philosophy. The sous with holes bored in them, the talismans, each man's souvenirs.

Dissertation on the moral dynamic. Of the virtue of the sacraments.

A tendency to mysticism since my childhood. My conversations with God.

CV

Of Obsession, of Possession, of Prayer and Faith.

The dynamic Ethic of Jesus.

Renan finds it ridiculous that Jesus should believe in the omnipotence, even over matter, of Prayer and Faith.

The sacraments are the modes of this dynamic.

Of the infamy of the press, a great obstacle to the development of the Beautiful.

The Jews who are *librarians* and bear witness to the *Redemption*.

CVI

All these imbecile bourgeois who ceaselessly utter the words: immoral, immorality, morality in art, and other idiotic phrases, make me think of Louise Villedieu, the five-franc whore, who, having accompanied me one day to the Louvre, where she had never been before, began blushing and covering her face with her hands. And as we stood before the immortal statues and pictures she kept plucking me by the sleeve and asking how they could exhibit such indecencies in public.

The fig-leaves of Mr. Nieuwerkerke.

CVII

In order that the law of Progress could exist each man would have to be willing to enforce it; for it is only when every individual has made up his mind to move forward that humanity will be in a state of progress.

This hypothesis may serve to show that two contradictory ideas—free-will and destiny—are identical. Not only will there be identity between free-will and destiny in Progress, but this identity has always existed. This identity is history—the history of nations and individuals.

CVIII

A sonnet to be quoted in *My Heart Laid Bare*. Quote also the poem on Roland:

> I dreamt that night that Philis had returned
> Fair as she was in the brightness of day,
> And I desired once again to possess her as ghost
> And, like Ixion, to embrace a cloud.
>
> Her naked shadow stole into my bed,
> Saying, "Dear Damon, see, I have come back;
> Only grown fairer in my sad abode
> Where fate has held me since my departure.
>
> "I am come to kiss again the most beautiful of lovers;
> I am come to die again within thine embrace."
> Then, when my idol had abused my flame,

She said, "Adieu. I must return to the dead.
As thou hast bragged of having —— my body,
So also canst thou boast of having —— my soul."

PARNASSE SATYRIQUE

I believe that this sonnet is by Maynard.
Malassis pretends that it is by Théophile.

CIX

Hygiene. Projects. The more one desires, the stronger one's will.

The more one works, the better one works and the more one wants to work.

The more one produces, the more fecund one becomes.

After a debauch, one feels oneself always to be more solitary, more abandoned.

In the moral as in the physical world, I have been conscious always of an abyss, not only of the abyss of sleep, but of the abyss of action, of day-dreaming, of recollection, of desire, of regret, of remorse, of the beautiful, of number . . . etc.

I have cultivated my hysteria with delight and terror. Now I suffer continually from vertigo, and to-day, 23rd of January, 1862, I have received a singular warning, I have felt the wind of the wing of madness pass over me.

CX

Hygiene. Morality. To Honfleur! as soon as possible, before I sink further.

How many have been the presentiments and signs sent me already by God that it is *high time* to act, to consider the present moment as the most important of all moments and to take for my *everlasting delight* my accustomed torment, that is to say, my work!

CXI

Hygiene. Conduct. Morality. We are weighed down, every moment, by the conception and the sensation of Time. And there are but two means of escaping and forgetting this nightmare: Pleasure and work. Pleasure consumes us. Work strengthens us. Let us choose.

The more we employ one of these means, the more the other will inspire us with repugnance.

One can only forget Time by making use of it.

Nothing can be accomplished save by degrees.

De Maistre and Edgar Poe have taught me to reason.

No task seems long but that which one dares not begin. It becomes a nightmare.

CXII

Hygiene. In putting off what one has to do, one runs the risk of never being able to do it. In refusing instant conversion one risks damnation.

To heal all things, wretchedness, disease or melancholy, absolutely nothing is required but an *inclination* for work.

CXIII

Precious notes. Do, every day, what duty and prudence dictate.

If you worked every day your life would be more supportable. Work *six* days without relaxing.

To find subjects, Γνωθί σεαυτόν.

Always be a poet, even in prose.

The grand style (nothing more beautiful than the commonplace).

First make a start, then apply logic and analysis. Every hypothesis demands a conclusion.

To achieve a daily madness.

CXIV

Hygiene. Conduct. Morality. Two parts. Debts. (Ancelle.)

Friends (my mother, friends, myself).

Thus, 1,000 francs should be divided into two parts

of 500 francs each, and the second divided into three parts.

At Honfleur. To go through and classify all my letters (two days) and all my debts (two days). (Four categories: *notes of hand, large debts, small debts, friends.*) A classification of my engravings (two days). A classification of my notes (two days).

CXV

Hygiene. Morality. Conduct. Too late, perhaps!— My mother and Jeanne—My health, for pity's, for duty's sake!—The maladies of Jeanne. My mother's infirmities and loneliness.

To do one's duty every day and trust in God for the morrow.

The only method of earning money is to work in a disinterested manner.

A summary of wisdom. Toilet. Prayer. Work.

Prayer: charity, wisdom and strength.

Without charity I am no more than a resounding cymbal.

My humiliations have been the graces of God.

My phase of egoism—is it passed?

The faculty of being able to meet the need of the moment; exactitude, in other words, must infallibly obtain its reward.

*Prolonged unhappiness has upon the soul the same effect
as old age upon the body: one cannot stir, one takes to
one's bed. . . .*

*Extreme youth, on the other hand, finds reasons for
procrastination; when there is plenty of time to spare, one
is persuaded that years may be allowed to pass before one
need play one's part.*

CHATEAUBRIAND

CXVI

Hygiene. Conduct. Morality. Jeanne 300, my mother
200, myself 300—800 francs a month. To work from
six o'clock in the morning, fasting at midday. To work
blindly, without aim, like a madman. We shall see the
result.

I believe that I stake my destiny upon hours of uninterrupted work.

All may be redeemed. There is still time. Who
knows, even, if some new pleasure . . . ?

Fame, payment of my debts. Wealth of Jeanne and
my mother.

I have never yet tasted the pleasure of an accomplished
design.

Power of the fixed idea, power of hope.

The habit of doing one's duty drives out fear.

One must desire to dream and know how to dream.
The evocation of inspiration. A magic art. To sit down at
once and write. I reason too much.

Immediate work, even when it is bad, is better than day-dreaming.

A succession of small acts of will achieves a large result.

Every defeat of the will forms a portion of lost matter. How wasteful, then, is hesitation! One may judge this by the immensity of the final effort necessary to repair so many losses.

The man who says his evening prayer is a captain posting his sentinels. He can sleep.

Dreams and warnings of death.

Up to the present I have only enjoyed my memories alone; I must enjoy them in the company of another. To make the pleasures of the spirit one's passion.

Because I can understand the nature of a glorious existence, I believe myself capable of its realization. Oh, Jean-Jacques!

Work engenders good habits, sobriety and chastity, from which result health, riches, continuous and strengthening inspiration and charity. *Age quod agis.*

Fish, cold baths, showers, moss, pastilles occasionally, together with the abstinence from all stimulants.

Iceland moss . . . 125 grammes.

White sugar . . . 250 grammes.

Soak the moss for twelve to fifteen hours in a sufficient quantity of cold water, then pour off the water.

101

Boil the moss in two litres of water upon a slow and consant fire until these two litres are reduced to one, skim the froth off once, then add the 250 grammes of sugar and let it thicken to the consistency of syrup. Let it cool off. Take *three* very large tablespoonfuls daily, in the morning, at midday and in the evening. One need not be afraid to increase the doses if the crises are too frequent.

CXVII

Hygiene. Conduct. Method. I swear to observe henceforth the following rules as immutable rules of my life:

To pray every morning to God, *the source of all power and all justice; to my father, to Mariette and to Poe,* as intercessors; that they may give me the necessary strength to fulfil all my appointed tasks and that they may grant my mother a *sufficient span of life* in which to enjoy my transformation; to work all day long, or *as long,* at any rate, *as my strength allows me;* to put my trust in God, that is, in Justice itself, for the success of my plans; to offer, every evening, a further prayer, asking God for life and strength for my mother and myself; to divide all my earnings into four parts—one for current expenses, one for my creditors, one for my friends and one for my mother—to obey the strictest principles of sobriety, the first being the abstinence from all stimulants whatsoever.

A Selection of Consoling Maxims

upon

Love

Whoever writes maxims likes to exaggerate his character—the young pretend to be old, the old paint their faces.

Since the world, this vast system of contradictions, holds all forms of decay in great esteem—quick, let us darken our wrinkles; let us garland our hearts like a frontispiece, for sentiment is widely fashionable.

To what purpose? If you are no true men, be at least true animals. Be unaffected, and you will, of necessity, be useful or agreeable to somebody. Were my heart on my right side, it would find at least a thousand co-pariahs among the three thousand millions of beings who browse upon the nettles of sentiment.

If I begin with Love, it is because Love is for everyone —and they will deny it in vain—the greatest thing in life!

All you who feed some insatiable vulture—you Hoffmannesque poets, whom the harmonica sends dancing through crystal regions, whom the violin lacerates like a blade searching the heart—you eager and embittered on-lookers in whom the spectacle of nature herself promotes dangerous ecstasies; let Love be your *calmative*.

You tranquil, you *objective* poets, the noble partisans of technique, architects of style—you prudent ones who have a daily task to accomplish; let Love be your stimulant, an exhilarating and strengthening potion, and the gymnastic of pleasure your perpetual encouragement to action! To those the soporifics, to these the alcohols.

You for whom nature is cruel and time precious; let Love be a burning draught which inspires the soul.

It is necessary, therefore, to choose one's loves.

Without denying the *coups de foudre,* which is impossible—see Stendhal (*De l'Amour*—book one, chapter XXIII)—one must suppose that fate possesses a certain elasticity, which is called human liberty.

In the same way as, for theologians, liberty consists in avoiding occasions of temptation rather than in resisting it; so, in Love, liberty consists in avoiding women of a dangerous category—dangerous, that is to say, for yourself.

Your mistress, the woman of your paradise, will be sufficiently indicated to you by your natural sympathies, verified by Lavater and by a study of painting and statuary.

The physiognomical signs would be infallible if one

knew them all, and well. I cannot here set down all the physiognomical signs of the woman eternally suitable to such and such a man. Perhaps one day I shall accomplish this enormous task in a book which will be entitled: *the catechism of the beloved woman;* but I am certain that every man, assisted by his imperious and vague desires and guided by observation, can discover, after a time, the woman necessary to himself. Further, our sympathies are not, in general, dangerous; nature, whether in cookery or in love, rarely gives us a taste for what is bad for us.

As I understand the word Love in its fullest sense, I am here obliged to set down some special maxims upon delicate questions.

You man of the North, you eager navigator lost in the mists, seeker of auroras more beautiful than the sunlight, untiring in your thirst for the ideal; love cold women. Love them well, for the toil is greater and more bitter and you will find one day more honour at the tribunal of Love, who is seated over there in the blue of the infinite!

You man of the South, you whose open nature can have no taste for secrets and mysteries—light-hearted man—of Bordeaux, of Marseilles or of Italy—let passionate women suffice you; their mobility and their animation are your natural empire, an empire of beguilement.

Young man, you who wish to become a great poet, be-

ware of the paradoxical in Love; let schoolboys excited by
their first pipe sing at the top of their voice the praises of
the fat women; leave these falsehoods to the neophytes of
the pseudo-romantic school. If the fat woman is sometimes a charming caprice, the thin woman is a well of
sombre delights!

Never slander great Nature; if she has bestowed upon
you a mistress without a bosom, say: "I have a love—
with such hips!" and go to the temple to render thanks
to the Gods.

You must know how to make the best of ugliness
itself—of your own, that is too easy—everyone knows
how Trenk (*la gueule brûlée*) was adored by women; *
of hers! that is a rarer and more beautiful art, but the
association of ideas will render it easy and natural. Let us
suppose that your idol is ill. Her beauty has disappeared
under the frightful crust of small-pox, like verdure beneath the heavy winter ice. Still shaken by long hours of
anguish and the fluctuations of the disease, you are regarding sorrowfully the ineffaceable stigmata upon the
body of the dear convalescent; then suddenly there vi-
brates in your ears a *dying* air executed by the rapturous
bow of Paganini, and this air speaks to you with sym-

* We could have cited Mirabeau as an example, but he is
too well known; besides, we suspect that he had a full-blooded
type of ugliness which is particularly distasteful to us.

pathy of yourself, seeming to reiterate the whole poem of your dearest abandoned hopes. Thenceforward, the traces of the small-pox will form a part of your happiness, beneath your tender gaze there will always echo the mysterious air of Paganini. Henceforth they will be the objects, not only of sweet sympathy but even of physical desire—if, that is, you are one of those sensitive spirits for whom beauty is the *promise* of happiness. Above all, it is an association of ideas which makes one love ugly women—so much so that you run a grave risk, if your pockmarked mistress betrays you, of being able to console yourself only with pock-marked women.

For certain spirits, more precious and more jaded, delight in ugliness proceeds from a still more obscure sentiment—the thirst for the unknown and the taste for the horrible. It is this sentiment, whose germ, more or less developed, is carried within each one of us, which drives certain poets into the dissecting room or the clinic and women to public executions. I am sincerely sorry for the man who cannot understand this—he is a harp who lacks a bass string!

As for illiteracy, which forms (according to some blockheads) a part of moral ugliness—is it not superfluous to explain to you how this may be a whole naïve poem of memories and delights? The charming Alcibiades lisped so well; childhood has such a divine jargon.

Then beware, young adept of pleasure, of teaching your
love French—unless it is necessary to become her French
master that you may be her lover.

There are those who blush to have loved a woman as
soon as they perceive that she is stupid. These are vain-
glorious jackasses, born to crop the foulest thistles in
creation or enjoy the favours of a blue-stocking. Stupidity
is often an ornament of beauty; it gives the eyes that
mournful limpidity of dusky pools, and that oily calm
of tropical seas. Stupidity always preserves beauty, it
keeps away the wrinkles, it is the divine cosmetic which
preserves our idols from the gnawings of thought which
we must suffer, miserable scholars that we are.

There are those who begrudge their mistress's extravagance. These are the misers, republicans ignorant of the
first principles of political economy. The vices of a great
nation are its greatest wealth.

There are others, the sedate, the reasonable, moderate
deists, followers of the middle path in dogma, who are
furious when their wives become devout. Oh! the fum-
blers, who will never learn to play any instrument! Oh,
the thrice-foolish ones, who do not perceive that the most
adorable form religion can take—is that of their wife! A
husband to be converted, what a delicious apple! The
beautiful fruit forbidden like some huge impiety—on a
stormy winter night, in a corner by the fire, with wine

and truffles—mute hymn of domestic bliss, victory over harsh Nature, who seems herself to be blaspheming the gods!

I should not have finished so soon had I wished to enumerate all the beautiful and noble aspects of what is called vice and moral ugliness, but there is one problem which often presents itself to men of feeling and understanding, a problem as vexed and painful as a tragic drama; it is when they are caught between the hereditary moral impulse implanted by their parents and the tyrannical desire for a woman whom they ought to despise. Numerous and ignoble infidelities, habits which betray their evil haunts, shameful secrets unseasonably laid bare, inspire you with horror for your idol, and it sometimes comes to pass that your joy makes you shudder. Here you are much embarrassed in your platonic reasonings. Virtue and Pride cry: Fly from her. Nature speaks in your ear: whither can I fly? These are terrible alternatives, in face of which even the strongest souls reveal the insufficiency of all our philosophic education. The more cunning, seeing themselves constrained by nature to play the eternal drama of Manon Lescaut and Leone Leoni, make their retreat, saying that contempt goes well with love. I am going to give you a very simple formula which will not only save you from these shameful self-justifications but will make it possible for you even to leave your idol undisfigured, without injury to your *crystallization*.*

We will suppose that the heroine of your heart has abused the *fas* and *nefas* and is come to the limits of perdition, after having—final infidelity! supreme torture!—tried the power of her charms upon her gaolers and executioners.† Are you going to abjure your ideal so lightly, or, if nature throws you, faithful and weeping, into the arms of this pale victim of the guillotine, will you say, with the mortified accents of resignation: Contempt and Love are cousins-german? Not at all. These are the paradoxes of a timid nature and a clouded intelligence. Say boldly and with the candour of the true philosopher: "Had she been less criminal my ideal had been less complete. I contemplate her and I submit; great Nature alone knows what she intends to make of such a glorious hussy. Supreme happiness and supreme absolute reason! product of contrary forces. Ormuz and Ahriman, you are one!"

And thus, thanks to a more synthetic outlook upon things, your admiration will lead you quite naturally towards chaste love, that sunlight in whose intensity all stains are swallowed up.

Remember this, that one must beware above all of the paradoxical in love. It is simplicity which saves, it is simplicity which brings happiness, though your mistress be as ugly as old Mab, the queen of terrors. In general, for

* We know that all our readers have read their Stendhal.
† Also *L'Ane Mort*.

men of the world, a subtle moralist has said, Love is but love of gambling, love of fighting. That is altogether wrong. Love should be love, fighting and gambling are permissible only as the politics of love.

The gravest mistake of modern youth is that they *force* their emotions. A great number of lovers are imaginary invalids who spend large sums on nostrums and pay M. Fleurant and M. Purgon heavily, without enjoying the pleasures and privileges of a genuine malady. Observe how they irritate their stomachs with absurd drugs, wearing out the digestive faculties of Love. It may be necessary to belong to one's century, but beware of apeing the illustrious Don Juan, who was, according to Molière, at first nothing more than a rude rascal, well trained and versed in love, crime and cunning, but who has since become, thanks to MM. Alfred de Musset and Théophile Gautier, an artistic lounger, chasing perfection through the bawdy-houses, and who is finally only an old dandy worn out by his travels, the stupidest creature in the world when he is in the company of an honest woman who loves her husband.

A last, general rule: in love, beware of the *moon* and the *stars,* beware of the Venus de Milo, of lakes, guitars, rope-ladders, and of all love stories—yes, even the most beautiful in the world, were it written by Apollo himself! But love dearly, vigorously, fearlessly, orientally, ferociously the woman you love; so that your love—harmony being included—does not torment the love of another; so that your choice does not cause disturbance to the community. Among the Incas a man could make love to his sister; be content with your cousin. Do not climb balconies or give trouble to the public authorities; do not on any account deprive your mistress of the happiness of belief in the gods; and when you accompany her to the temple remember to dip your fingers in orthodox fashion in the pure, refreshing water of the stoup.

Since all morality testifies to the good will of its legislators—since all religion is a supreme consolation for the afflicted—since every woman is a part of *essential* Woman—since love is the sole thing which merits the turning of a sonnet and the putting-on of fine linen: I revere these things above all else and denounce as a slanderer the man who sees in this fragment of a morality an occasion for crossing himself and a cause for scandal. Morality wrapped in tinsel, is it not? Coloured glass which tints too brightly, perhaps, the eternal lamp of truth shining within? No, no. Had I wished to prove that all is for the best in the best of all possible worlds, the reader would have the right to tell me, like the *ape of genius:* you are naughty! But I have desired to prove that all is for the best in the worst of all possible worlds. Much therefore will be forgiven me because I have loved much—my male, or female reader!

CITY LIGHTS PUBLICATIONS